Short Walks in West Sussex

David Weller

COUNTRYSIDE BOOKS
NEWBURY BERKSHIRE

First published 2024
© 2024 David Weller

All rights reserved. No part of this publication may be reproduced, stored in a retrieval system, or transmitted by any means, electronic, mechanical, photocopying, recording or otherwise, without the prior written permission of the copyright holder and publishers.

COUNTRYSIDE BOOKS
3 Catherine Road
Newbury, Berkshire, RG14 7NA

To view our complete range of books please visit us at
www.countrysidebooks.co.uk

ISBN 978 1 84674 429 7

All materials used in the manufacture of this book carry FSC certification.

Produced by The Letterworks Ltd., Reading
Designed and Typeset by KT Designs, St Helens
Printed by Holywell Press, Oxford

Introduction

West Sussex is such a lovely county with its wonderful mosaic of habitats and its extensive network of footpaths, bridleways and cart tracks making it easy to explore on foot. From the seashore of the coastal region to both the High and Low Wealds inland; the full majesty of the county is displayed and then, to top it all, running through the centre of the county is its 'jewel in the crown' – the South Downs National Park.

This collection of short circular walks will lead you easily through this splendid variety of habitats and will demonstrate the diversity of the West Sussex countryside. Where possible I have selected routes that begin from car parks; some are pay and display while others are free but, it is inevitable that some walks require roadside parking so please park responsibly.

Whether walking alone or with family, it is always a great pleasure passing through this wonderful landscape. Some of the terrain underfoot may be slippery or uneven so I recommend you wear good walking boots or

Short Walks in West Sussex

shoes and to accompany the sketch maps, I have recommended the relevant OS map that will give you a better understanding of the surrounding area.

I would remind walkers of the famous quote from Indian Chief Seattle (c1786 – 1866), *'take nothing but memories; leave nothing but footprints'*.

Enjoy your walking!

David Weller

Publisher's Note

We hope that you obtain considerable enjoyment from this book; great care has been taken in its preparation. Although at the time of publication all routes followed public rights of way or permitted paths, diversion orders can be made and permissions withdrawn.

We cannot, of course, be held responsible for such diversion orders or any inaccuracies in the text which result from these or any other changes to the routes, nor any damage which might result from walkers trespassing on private property. We are anxious, though, that all the details covering the walks are kept up to date, and would therefore welcome information from readers which would be relevant to future editions.

The simple sketch maps that accompany the walks in this book are based on notes made by the author whilst surveying the routes on the ground. They are designed to show you how to reach the start and to point out the main features of the overall circuit, and they contain a progression of numbers that relate to the paragraphs of the text.

However, for the benefit of a proper map, we do recommend that you purchase the relevant Ordnance Survey sheet covering your walk. Ordnance Survey maps are widely available, especially through booksellers and local newsagents.

1 South Harting & its environs

2¼ miles (3.6 km)

Start: South Harting village, where there is roadside parking in The Street near The White Hart. **Postcode:** GU31 5QB.
OS Map: OL8 Chichester. **Grid Ref:** SU785195.
Terrain: Fairly level with just one short easy hill. **Stiles:** None.
Refreshments: The White Hart, GU31 5QB. ☎ 01730 825124.
🌐 www.the-whitehart.co.uk

WALK HIGHLIGHTS

This super walk begins in the centre of the lovely old village of South Harting that is tucked up against the border of Hampshire. Within a very short distance of passing the village stocks and whipping post, the route crosses scenic open fields, all the while with a backdrop of the South Downs in the distance. Field paths are the order of the day here as the route circles

Short Walks in West Sussex

the northern environs of the village before returning to its centre, passing a variety of houses, some modern and others centuries old.

THE WALK

❶ From where you have parked, walk towards the **Church of St Mary & St Gabriel** and turn right beside the **village stocks** and **whipping post**. Follow this short track to the gate of **Church Farm** and then go right on a fenced path to soon meet a driveway. Go right along the drive to meet a road.

❷ Cross the road to the grassy path opposite and press on ahead between fields with panoramic views. When the path ends at a country lane, turn right along the lane to meet a T-junction.

❸ Here turn right along the pavement for 50 metres before crossing the road to a signed footpath. Now follow a fenced path to meet a field. Go ahead alongside this field. Along the way the path goes through the hedgerow and continues along the right side of the next field. Ignore a path signed to your left and press on down a slope. Pass through a line of trees to meet an open grassy area near a **Water Works**. Follow the grassy path uphill alongside the works access drive to meet a track.

Walk 1 – South Harting & its environs

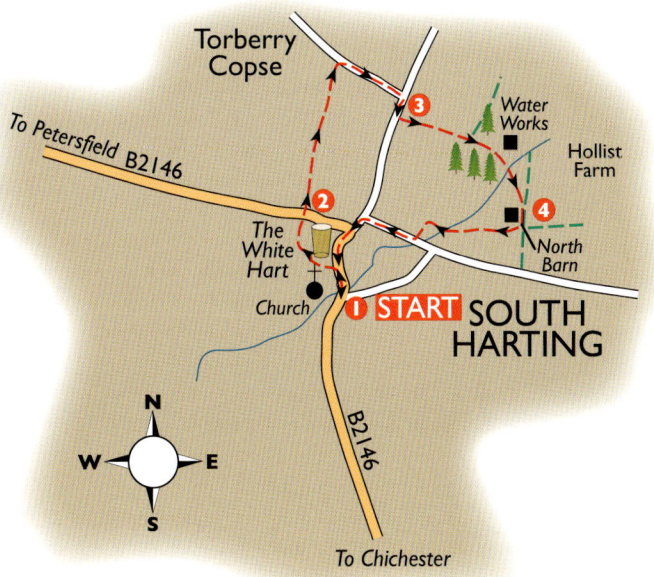

4 Go right here passing **North Barn** and **Kent House**. Soon look out for a signed crossing path. Go right through a gate, cross a field and pass through a second gate and field. At the field end, go down a slope to meet a quiet country lane. Turn left along the lane to soon meet the village street where a right turn leads back to the village centre.

2 West Itchenor & the Chichester Channel

2½ miles (4km)

Start: Chichester Harbour Conservancy Car Park, just off The Street in Itchenor village. **Postcode:** PO20 7AH.
OS Map: OL8 Chichester. **Grid Ref:** SU797013.
Terrain: Level. **Stiles:** 1, dog friendly.
Refreshments: The Ship Inn, Itchenor, PO20 7AH. ☎ 01243 512284.
🌐 www.theshipinnitchenor.co.uk.

WALK HIGHLIGHTS

West Itchenor has a long history dating back to when the Anglo-Saxon chieftain Icca resided here and it became known as Icca's shore, later Iccanore which is not far away from its modern name. East Itchenor had ceased to exist by the 15th century. Leaving history behind, this lovely walk begins in the village centre where traffic is light. As the route leaves the

Walk 2 – West Itchenor & the Chichester Channel

village, it passes the grounds of Itchenor Park House to reach level fields where the way leads easily to the shoreline of the Chichester Channel. What follows is a path that traces the water's edge giving extensive views across the waterway before finally ending back at the village.

THE WALK

❶ From the car park, walk back to **The Street** and turn right along it. Now follow this quiet road for ¼ mile (.4km) passing individually designed houses. At a left bend the driveway to **Itchenor Park House & Farm** will be seen to the right.

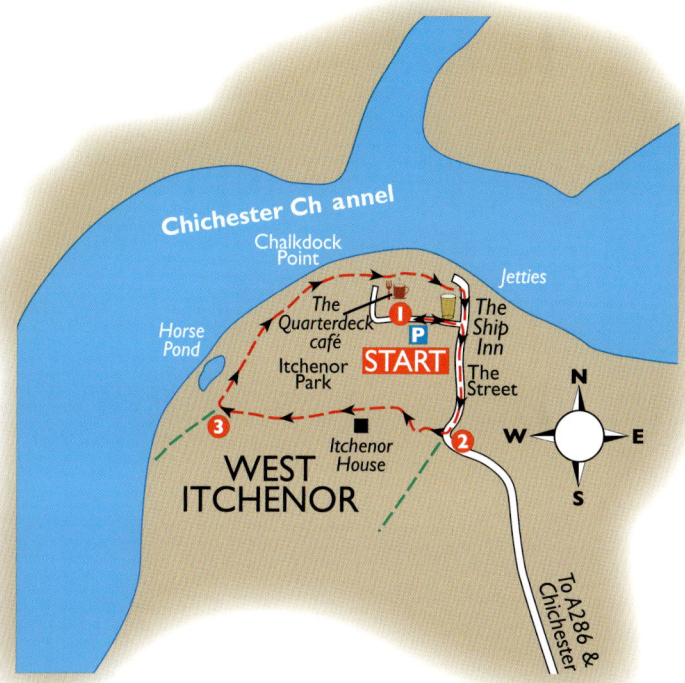

Short Walks in West Sussex

2 Turn right along this drive and when at the gate of **Itchenor Park House**, follow the drive rightwards. Soon continue on a footpath between a low wall and a field fence. Cross a low stile at its end to meet a concrete drive. Turn left along the drive and when that ends, keep ahead on a cart track. At a gate across the cart track fork slightly right and maintain direction ahead along a field edge.

3 At the field end, pass through a squeeze stile to meet a T-junction. Turn right here on the well-trodden path and follow it for 1 mile (1.6km). As the path nears the village, go ahead through a boatyard where **The Quarterdeck** café will be passed to your right. Keep ahead on a narrow path; pass the **Harbour Office** in **Itchenor Harbour** to meet **The Street**. Turn right along the road and pass **The Ship Inn** to rejoin the car park entrance and the end of the walk.

3 Kingley Vale & Stoke Down

2 miles (3.2km)

Start: West Stoke Car Park, a National Nature Reserve car park just off Downs Road in Kingley Vale. **Postcode:** PO18 9BE.
OS Map: OL8 Chichester. **Grid Ref:** SU825088.
Terrain: There is one long low easy rise, otherwise fairly level.
  Stiles: None.
Refreshments: The Horse & Groom, East Ashling, PO18 9AX.
☎ 01243 575339. ⊕ www.thehorseandgroom.pub

WALK HIGHLIGHTS

Not only is this an easy walk to follow but it leads you through some of the best downland scenery the county can offer. The route begins by following a lovely track between fields that leads to the gate of Kingley Vale National Nature Reserve. You can of course visit the reserve but be aware the paths

Short Walks in West Sussex

are steep. Avoiding these steep paths the way turns and crosses Stoke Down via a bridleway that offers stunning views across the downland. This wonderful bridleway then continues through the coolness of West Copse before ending at a quiet country lane that returns you to the car park.

THE WALK

❶ Leave the car park from the end furthest from its entrance. Pass an information board and go through a kissing gate to meet a wide track. Now follow this track for ¾ mile (1.2km) until it ends by the gate to **Kingley Vale National Nature Reserve**.

❷ Ignore the gate and turn left here on a bridleway that soon divides. Keep ahead on the left fork and follow the slowly rising bridleway across a landscape that is known for its Neolithic and Bronze Age finds. Later the bridleway passes through **West Copse** before finally ending at a country lane.

Walk 3 – **Kingley Vale & Stoke Down**

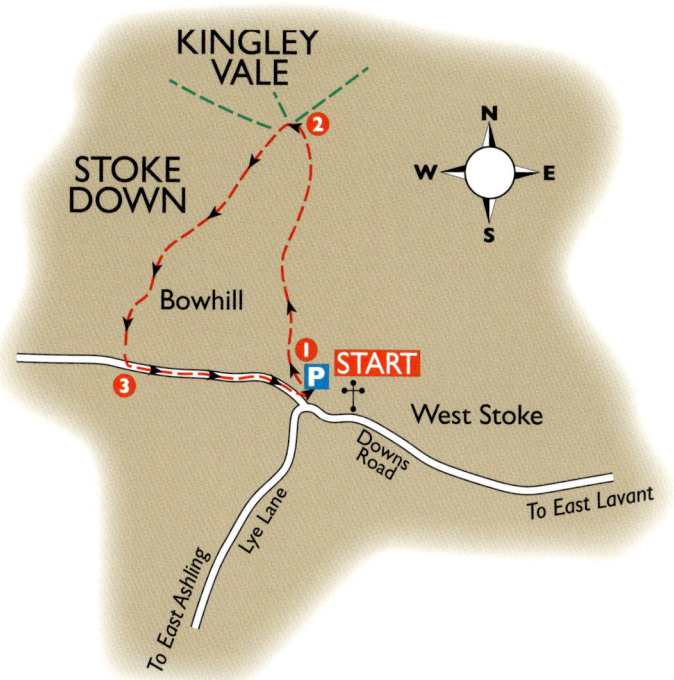

③ Turn left along this quiet country lane that will return you to the car park in ½ mile (.8km) to end this scenic route.

4 East Beach & the salad fields of Selsey

3 miles (4.8km)

Start: East Beach Car Park (pay and display, toilets available), off Beach Road. **Postcode:** PO20 0SZ.
OS Map: OL8 Chichester. **Grid Ref:** SZ866934.
Terrain: Level. **Stiles:** None.
Refreshments: East Beach Kiosk & Paddy's Plaice, PO20 0SZ.
☎ 01243 602496. ⊕ No website.

WALK HIGHLIGHTS

This engaging circuit begins in the South Coast's least developed seaside resort; no kiss me quick hats here, although you can indulge in fish and chips on the promenade. After following the promenade for a short distance the way continues along a track lined by an eclectic assortment of seafront homes, some built around railway carriages. After leaving them behind,

Walk 4 – East Beach & the salad fields of Selsey

the route continues along the shingle beach before heading inland beside salad growing fields. Wide tracks then lead you back to the promenade from where it is just a short walk back to the car park and the end of this good walk.

THE WALK

❶ Leave the car park at the end furthest from the entrance to meet the promenade and turn left along it until it ends. Here turn left and in

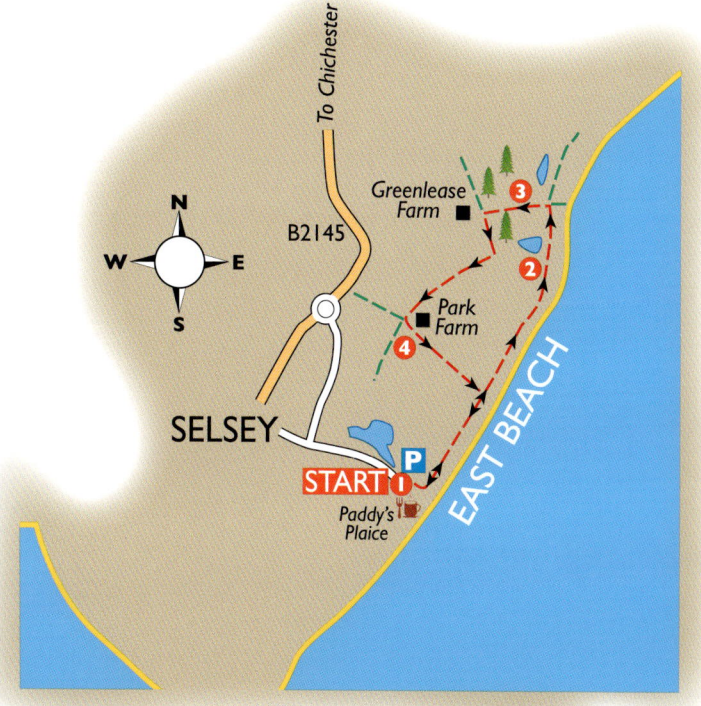

Short Walks in West Sussex

15 metres turn right along an unmade wide track signed as the **England Coast Path**.

❷ After passing a collection of seaside homes, the way continues ahead along the top of the shingle bank. Look out for a **wildlife pond** that is soon spotted to your left and fork left away from the shingle and continue on a grassy path to meet a crossing track.

❸ Turn left here; pass through woodland after which the path continues ahead alongside a growing field towards the buildings of **Greenlease Farm**. The path ends at a T-junction. Turn left here on the path as it skirts the end of the field and remain on it as it brings you to a wide track between fields. Keep ahead on the track until it ends at the buildings of **Park Farm**.

❹ Pass through a gate and ignore the track ahead of you. Turn left along the unmade track that eventually becomes tarmacked and meets the promenade where a right turn will deliver you back to the car park and the end of this good varied route.

5 Iping & Stedham Commons

3 miles (4.8km)

Start: Iping Common Car Park, off Elsted Road. **Postcode:** GU29 0PB.
OS Map: OL33 Haslemere & Petersfield. **Grid Ref:** SU852220.
Terrain: Undulating. **Stiles:** 2.
Refreshments: Plenty of eateries in nearby Midhurst.

WALK HIGHLIGHTS

This good, varied circuit starts and finishes at Iping & Stedham Commons that make up some of the best examples of low-land heath in Sussex. Managed by the Sussex Wildlife Trust, this declining habitat is a gem for wildlife and walkers alike. After crossing Stedham Common the way turns and passes through the pretty village of Stedham to meet the River Rother. Here the route follows its course for a short while before meeting and

Short Walks in West Sussex

passing by the hamlet of Iping. After following field paths the way makes its return across Iping Common before bringing the route to an end back at the car park.

THE WALK

❶ Walk back to the car park entrance, cross the road and pass through a gate. Ignore a path to the left and go ahead on a well-defined bridleway across **Stedham Common** until after ½ mile (.8km) a country lane is met.

❷ Turn left along the lane that soon ends at the **A272**. As you near the main road, veer right and cross the road via a central reservation. At the far side turn left to meet a small lane. Turn right here and follow this lane into the pretty village of **Stedham**.

❸ After passing the village green a fork in the road is met. Here keep left and 30 metres before meeting **Stedham Bridge** turn left on a signed bridleway initially alongside the **River Rother**.

The River Rother drove mills at both Stedham and Iping; the former making blotting paper and the latter printing paper.

Walk 5 – Iping & Stedham Commons

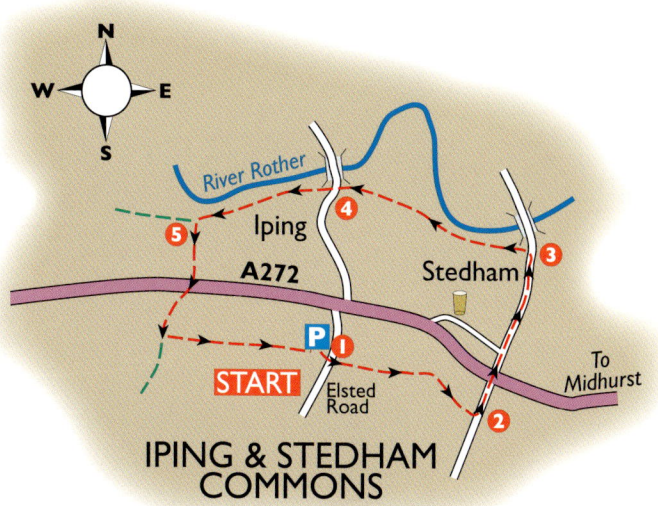

Keep to the well-defined bridleway that ends at a gate and driveway. Go ahead along the drive, pass **Coachman's Cottage** and follow the bridleway to meet a small lane.

❹ Ahead there are two driveways. Follow the signed footpath along the left-hand drive and very soon fork right on a narrow signed path. At woodland, keep to the path; cross a bridge over a brook and go ahead over a stile. Keep ahead along the right side of a field and at its top end cross a stile to meet a fingerpost.

❺ Go left here alongside a field passing through two kissing gates to meet a lane. Go ahead to meet the **A272** road. Turn left along the grass verge for 30 metres before crossing the road with caution to a signed bridleway. The bridleway initially goes rightwards before swinging left up a slope to meet a wide crossing track. Turn left on this wide track that after ½ mile (.8km) ends back at the car park.

6 Cocking Hill & Crypt Farm

1¾ miles (3.2km)

> **Start:** Cocking Hill Car Park, beside the A286. The entrance is at the top of the hill by a bus stop. **Postcode:** GU29 0HT.
> **OS Map:** OL8 Chichester. **Grid Ref:** SU875166.
> **Terrain:** One rise of 250ft (76m) over ¾ mile (1.2km) that is not beyond a person of average fitness. **Stiles:** None.
> **Refreshments:** The Blue Bell pub in Cocking, GU29 0HU.
> ☎ 01730 239669. ⊕ www.info@thebluebellatcocking.co.uk

WALK HIGHLIGHTS

This energetic and easy to follow short route begins on top of Cocking Hill and follows a section of the South Downs Way long-distance path along a track that climbs to the heights of Cocking Down. From here there are extensive panoramic views across the wonderful surrounding countryside. The route then turns and leaves the long-distance path via a bridleway that

Walk 6 – **Cocking Hill & Crypt Farm**

descends easily over fields and through woodland to reach the buildings of Crypt Farm. The way then follows a track on a short climb that leads you back to the car park.

THE WALK

1 Leave the car park by its northern end and turn left along the **South Downs Way** long-distance path. Pass by **Cadence Café** and the buildings of **Cocking Hill Farm**. Keep ahead along the rising stony track to meet a bridleway signed to left and right by a large ball of chalk.

This carved chalk ball measures 2 metres across and marks the start of a 5-mile walk called 'The Chalk Stones Trail' which ends at West Dean Gardens. The trail is marked by 12 more carved chalk balls and was created by Andy Goldsworthy, an environmental artist.

2 Turn hard right on the signed bridleway over **Cocking Down**. Note the direction indicated by the fingerpost as the bridleway is indistinct. Go down the slope and pass through a gap in the fence ahead by a second fingerpost. Now follow a narrow downhill path that begins slightly rightwards to meet a hedgerow. With the hedgerow close to your right, continue to the bottom corner of the field and pass through a gate.

3 Follow the bridleway as it passes through woodland to meet **Crypt Farm**. Go ahead alongside the buildings and when the drive bends left, go ahead on a rough track that soon bends right and goes uphill. Now follow this track that later narrows and returns you to the **South Downs Way** and **Cadence Café**. Turn left here to rejoin the car park.

Short Walks in West Sussex

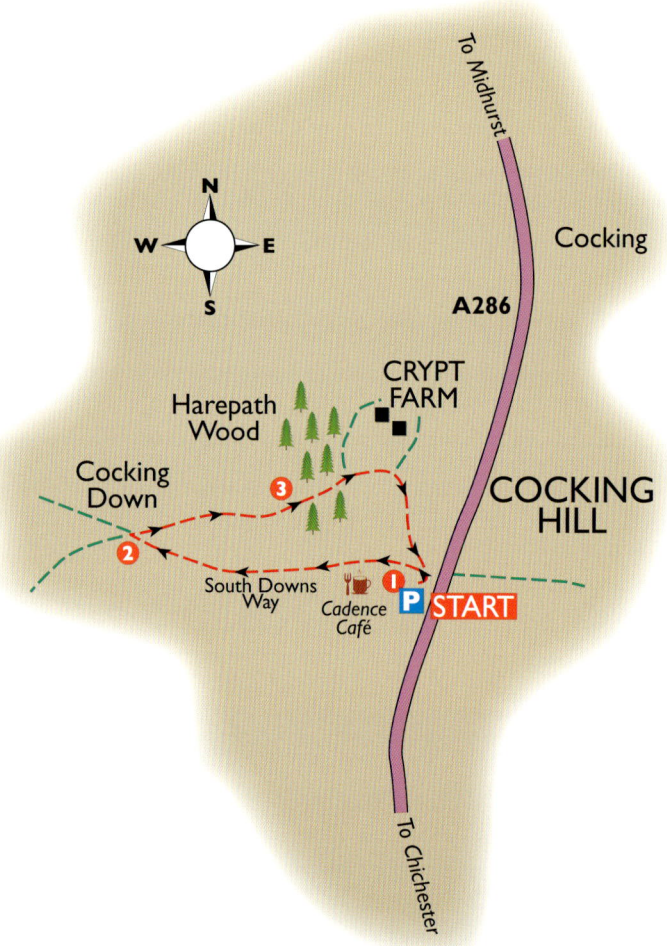

7 St Roche's Hill & the Monarch's Way

3 miles (4.8km)

Start: Trundle Car Park on St Roche's Hill, 1 mile past the Open Air Museum. **Postcode:** PO18 0SP.
OS Map: OL8 Chichester. **Grid Ref:** SU872110.
Terrain: The last mile (1.6km) has a steady rise of 280 feet that should not trouble a person of average fitness. **Stiles:** None.
Refreshments: The Selsey Arms, West Dean, PO18 0QX.
☎ 01243 811465. ⊕ www.selseyarms-westdean.co.uk

WALK HIGHLIGHTS

This easy to follow route can best be described in three words; views, views, views. The route begins on top of St Roche's Hill where the panorama across the countryside reaches as far as Chichester and the spire of its cathedral. The route begins by descending easily across Haye's Down to meet a path

Short Walks in West Sussex

in the Lavant Valley below. After following this path along the valley floor, the way meets the Monarch's Way long-distance path which the route then follows on a steady climb through glorious woodland to finally reach the top of St Roche's Hill and the end of this exhilarating walk.

THE WALK

❶ Walk back to the car park entrance and go ahead passing the gate to a large house. Continue ahead on a well-trodden path ignoring a right fork in 30 metres. Keep to this lovely path as it crosses **Haye's Down** and begins to descend to the valley below. Later the path passes through a gate and continues through a field to meet a gate beside a fingerpost at the foot of the slope.

❷ Do not go through the gate. Turn right here along the foot of the field and follow this path along the valley floor passing through a couple of gates along the way. Later ignore a path to the left and remain ahead to meet a T-junction by a stone wall.

Walk 7 – St Roche's Hill & the Monarch's Way

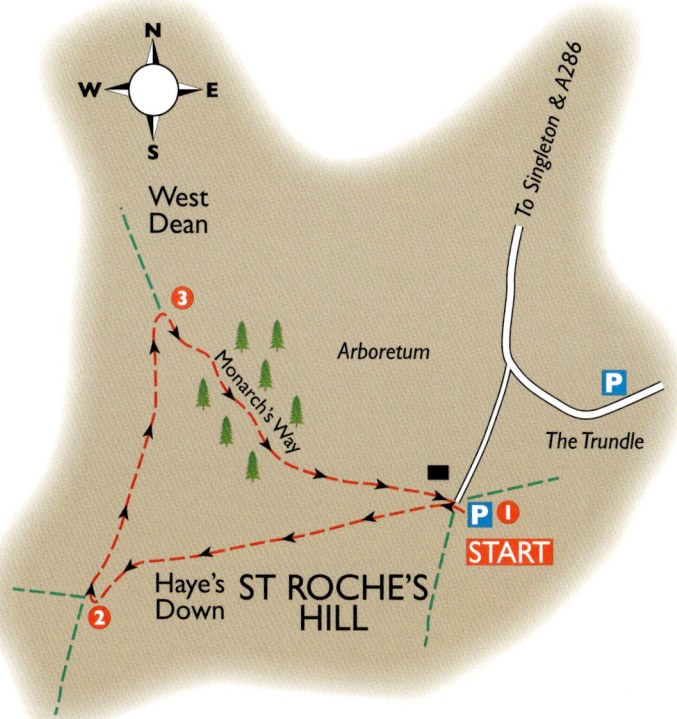

③ This is the **Monarch's Way** long-distance path and you should now turn right on the rising path that soon enters glorious woodland. Now follow the path until it emerges on top of St Roche's Hill where you should go ahead to rejoin the car park to complete this lovely circuit.

The Monarch's Way long-distance path follows the supposed escape route used by King Charles II in 1651 after his defeat in the Battle of Worcester. It begins in Worcester and ends at Shoreham-by-Sea.

8 Lurgashall, in the shadow of Blackdown

2¼ miles (3.6km)

Start: Lurgashall, beside the village green. **Postcode:** GU28 9ET.
OS Map: OL33 Haslemere & Petersfield. **Grid Ref:** SU937272.
Terrain: Gently undulating. **Stiles:** 5, none dog friendly.
Refreshments: The Noah's Ark Inn, GU28 9ET. ☎ 01428 707346.
🌐 www.noahsarkinn.co.uk

WALK HIGHLIGHTS

After leaving the pretty village of Lurgashall the path passes through small pastures to reach woodland. Here the way follows a path between the trees alongside the lower south-easterly slopes of Blackdown Hill; the highest point of the South Downs National Park. After emerging from woodland the way continues along field paths that offer panoramic views across the countryside. As the route nears its end it continues through the graveyard of the ancient church of St Laurence from where it rejoins the village green to complete this fine country walk.

Walk 8 – **Lurgashall, in the shadow of Blackdown**

THE WALK

1 From wherever you parked, go to the **Noah's Ark Inn** and when facing it, go left alongside the village green at the end of which turn right on a signed footpath. Keep to the path as it passes through a series of kissing gates and finally enters woodland. Go ahead on the well-trodden path until it ends at a stile.

2 Ignore a track to your left here, cross the stile and continue ahead on the left side of a field. At the field end, pass through a line of trees to meet two

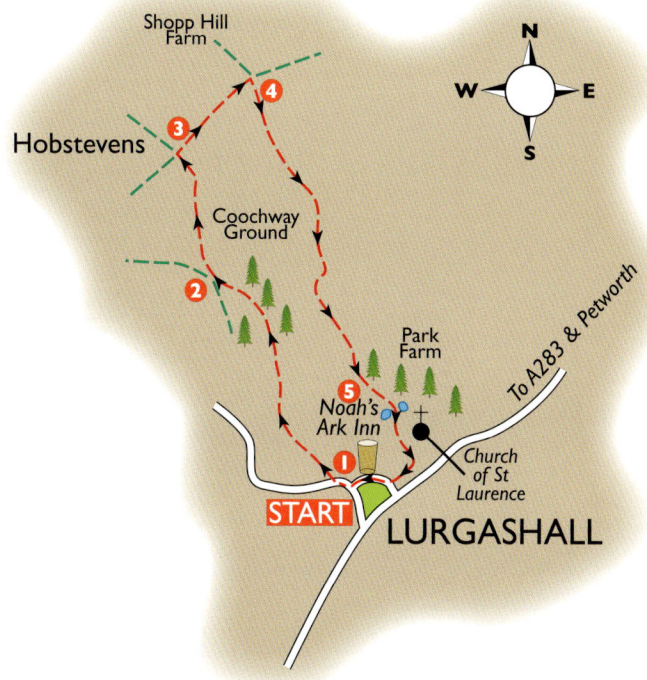

Short Walks in West Sussex

field gates. Go through the left-hand gate and continue along the left side of the field to meet a fingerpost and a stile.

❸ Do not cross the stile but turn right and follow a grassy path towards the bottom corner of the field. Seek out a signed path 20 metres to the left of the corner, pass through a gate and continue ahead to a second gate. Here, enter woodland and go down a slope with a handrail, cross a bridge and up steps at the far side to cross a stile. Press on along the right side of a field.

❹ At the field end, cross a stile on your right and follow a grassy path through the centre of a field to meet a gate at the far side. Pass through the gate and continue ahead through the next field to pass through a second gate to meet a farm track. Now turn right on the farm track and follow it for ½ mile (.8km) passing a **woodcraft centre**.

❺ Just before the track enters woodland, go left over a stile and follow the path and pass through a gate. Go ahead on a concrete drive to a T-junction. Turn right, pass between two ponds, at the end of which go left through a field gate. Press on along the left field edge, cross a stile and enter the graveyard of the **Church of St Laurence**. Now follow a short tarmac path to the right of the church to rejoin the village green and the end of this varied walk.

The church still retains some evidence that it dates from Saxon times but the wooden lean-to by its door is a survivor of the 15th century and is believed to have been divided into two: one end a schoolroom and the other a porch as it is today.

9 Burton Park & Duncton Mill

2¼ (3.6km)

Start: Park in the lay-by near the Cricketers pub, just off Duncton High Street/A285. **Postcode:** GU28 0LB.
OS Map: OL10 Arundel & Pulborough. **Grid Ref:** SU960169.
Terrain: One sharp 100ft (30m) rise that should not trouble a person of average fitness, otherwise fairly level. **Stiles:** None.
Refreshments: The Cricketers, GU28 0LB. ☎ 01798 342473.
⊕ www.thecricketersduncton.co.uk

WALK HIGHLIGHTS

This lovely route follows the driveway of Burton Park before crossing its extensive parkland and passing the house itself. The way then follows a bridleway that heads through Half Moon Copse where it passes the reflective waters of Chingford Pond. Continuing on, the walk then meets the

Short Walks in West Sussex

only hill on the route at Fountain Copse and it is from there that it is just a short distance to meet a quiet, traffic-free lane that passes Duncton Mill and its trout fishery before ending back at the lay-by.

THE WALK

❶ From the lay-by, cross the **A285** with caution to the pavement opposite and then turn right along it. Very soon, when opposite the ornate gates of **Burton Park** re-cross the road and go ahead along the drive. After passing through woodland a cattle grid is met. Go left here on a signed fenced path across open parkland to finally rejoin the drive.

❷ Turn hard right now and follow the drive with **Burton Park house** to your left.

19th-century Burton Park house is Grade I listed and was built in 1828 after the previous house was destroyed by fire. It is now apartments.

When the drive bends to the right; keep ahead on a grassy downhill bridleway towards a tree-line. Pass through an ornate gate and go ahead between two sections of **Chingford Pond**. Press on through a second gate and continue along the well-trodden path with a field either side.

Walk 9 – **Burton Park & Duncton Mill**

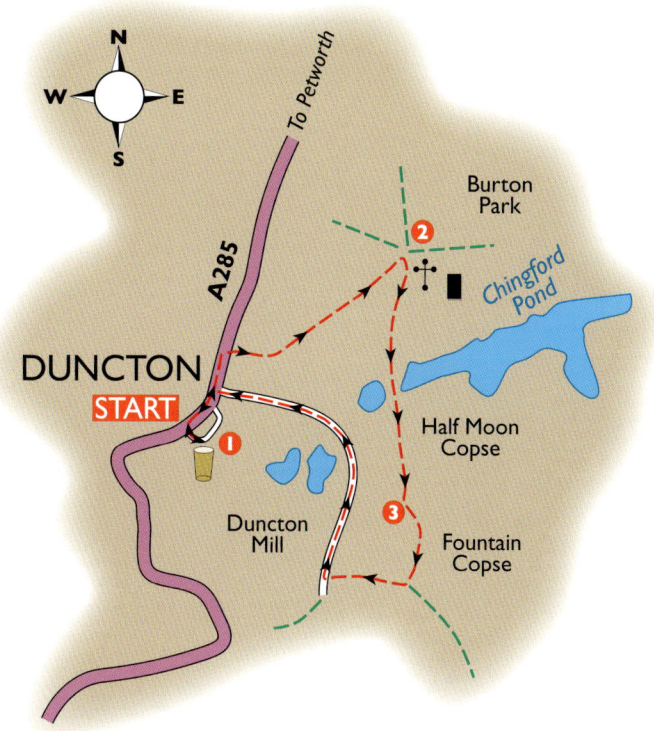

❸ At the field end, continue through a further gate and follow the path as it now rises quite steeply to meet a T-junction. Turn right here on a bridleway that soon meets with **Dye House Lane**. Turn right along this quiet lane, pass by **Duncton Mill Fishery** and remain on the lane until it ends in ½ mile (.8km) back at the **A285** with the lay-by just to the left.

10 Burpham & its environs

1½ miles (2.4km)

Start: The George pub in Burpham. Pass the front of the pub and park in the car park by the cricket ground. **Postcode:** BN18 9RR.
OS Map: OL10 Arundel & Pulborough. **Grid Ref:** TQ039089.
Terrain: Fairly level with one rise of 35ft (11m) over ¼ mile (.4km).
  Stiles: 1, dog friendly.
Refreshments: The George, BN18 9RR. ☎ 01903 883131.
🌐 www.georgeatburpham.co.uk

WALK HIGHLIGHTS

Burpham is an archetypical West Sussex village with rose bowered cottages, ancient church, community-owned pub and a cricket ground with wonderful views. The one thing though that sets it apart from most of the others is that it sits at the end of a dead end road and so does not suffer from through traffic. The walk begins by soon crossing wildflower meadows alongside the River Arun although the waterway remains unseen. After following the edge of open fields the route begins its return along a bridleway leading to Peppering Farm. From there it continues along a quiet lane with lovely views over the Arun Valley. As the way rejoins the village it passes St Mary's church just a few steps from the end of the walk.

Walk 10 – Burpham & its environs

THE WALK

1 From the car park, pass the front of **The George** pub and turn left on a lane that ends by a barn. Go ahead on a path between fences to meet a fork. Go right on a path that passes through woodland to meet a gate. Continue ahead on a grassy path that continues through two wildflower meadows.

2 When a cart track is met, go left along it and ignore a footpath signed left in 30 metres. As the cart track soon bends left, go ahead through a field gate and press on along the right side of a field. At the field end pass through a gap in the hedgerow, turn right to meet a fingerpost and then maintain your original direction along the right side of the field. At the field end cross a stile and enter another field, again keeping to the right side by the hedgerow.

3 50 metres before the field end, go right through a field gate to meet a cart track. Turn right and follow this track which contains the only slight hill on the route and offers panoramic views across the **Arun Valley**.

4 The track ends by **Peppering Farm**. Go ahead on a quiet lane that offers views as far as **Arundel Castle**. When a small green with seats is met, fork left on a path and enter the churchyard of **St. Mary's** where an unusually low window in the wall facing you can be seen.

This is a medieval leper's window that dates from around 1330 which allowed lepers to view the service from outside without coming into contact with worshippers.

Short Walks in West Sussex

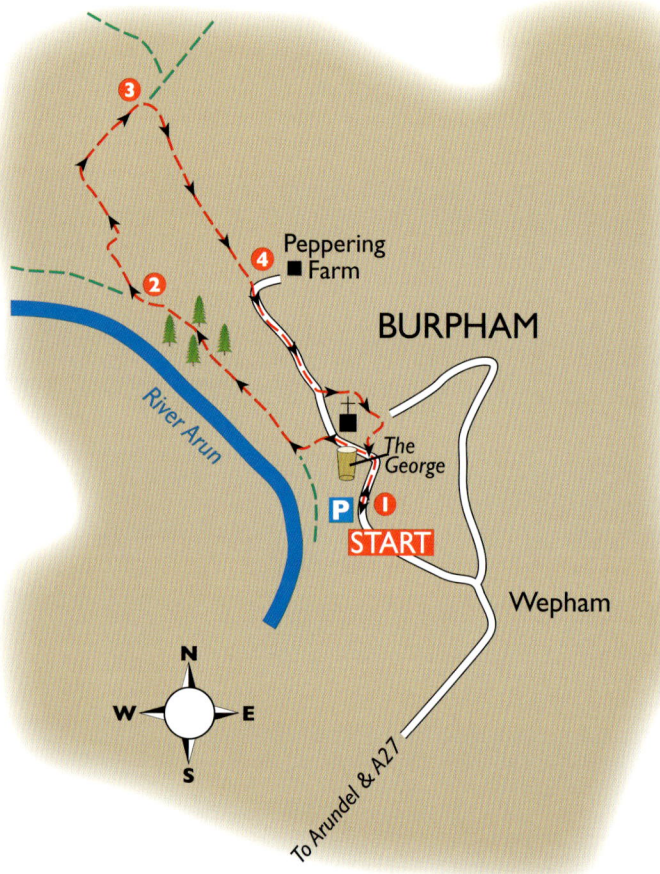

Continue ahead on the tarmac path to very soon pass **The George** pub to meet the car park.

11 The Wey & Arun Canal at Loxwood

4 miles (6.4km)

Start: The Wey & Arun Canal Visitor Centre beside the Onslow Arms pub. Park in the grassy area beyond the pub car park.
Postcode: RH14 0RD.
OS Map: OL34 Crawley & Horsham. **Grid Ref:** TQ042311.
Terrain: Level. **Stiles:** None.
Refreshments: The Onslow Arms, RH14 0RD. ☎ 01403 752022.
🌐 www.onslowarmsloxwood.com

WALK HIGHLIGHTS

This lovely level walk begins beside the Wey & Arun Canal Trust Visitor Centre which is handily next door to the Onslow Arms pub. After following the canal towpath westward, the way leaves the canal by Devil's Hole Lock bridge where the route then follows a well-trodden path across a scenic field to meet with a bridleway. Going north on this tree-lined bridleway the way meets a large crossing track that leads back to the canal towpath at Gennets Bridge Lock. From here the return is made along the towpath where parts illustrate just how the canal had attracted the name of 'London's lost route to the sea'.

Short Walks in West Sussex

THE WALK

❶ From the parking area, go to the **The Wey & Arun Trust Visitor Centre** to meet with the canal towpath. Turn left along the towpath passing the garden of **The Onslow Arms**. Press on through an underpass and go ahead along the towpath.

❷ After ½ mile (.8km) **Devil's Hole Lock** is reached. Here turn right over the bridge and follow a path away from the canal. Continue on a planked boardwalk to reach a field that is crossed via a well-trodden path towards a row of houses. The path passes alongside the houses to meet with a wide farm track marked as a bridleway.

❸ Turn left along the farm track and when it soon bends to the left, go ahead on the now narrower bridleway that passes through trees.

❹ Keep to the bridleway as it continues along a ribbon of trees and ignore the occasional footpaths to left and right and keep ahead at all times. Press on ahead when passing the ornate gateway to a large house. Finally the bridleway meets with a wide crossing track.

❺ Turn left here along this tree-lined track that soon delivers you back to the canal at **Gennets Wood Lock**. Cross the bridge and turn left along the towpath that will now lead you all the way back to complete this glorious route.

Walk 11 – **The Wey & Arun Canal at Loxwood**

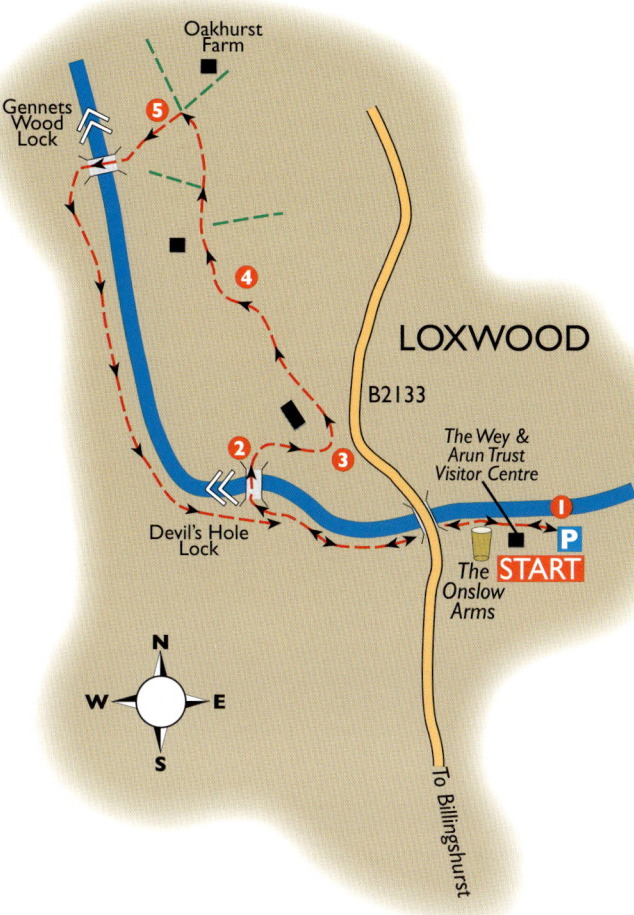

12 Kithurst Hill & the South Downs Way

1¾ (2.8km) or 2¾ (4.4km)

Start: Kithurst Hill car park. **Postcode:** RH20 4HW.
OS Map: OL10 Arundel & Pulborough. **Grid Ref:** TQ070124.
Terrain: Lightly undulating with just one very short, sharp hill on the longer route. **Stiles:** None.
Refreshments: The Anchor Inn, High Street, Storrington, RH20 4DU.
☎ 01903 742665. ⊕ www.theanchorstorrington.co.uk

WALK HIGHLIGHTS
This lovely scenic walk contains some of the best panoramic views that West Sussex can offer. To the north of the path are distant views over fields as

Walk 12 – **Kithurst Hill & the South Downs Way**

far as Storrington and beyond. The longer route continues to Chantry Hill where the path follows its rim, again with magnificent views. The route soon meets and follows the South Downs Way back to the car park. There is an easily followed shorter route available which cuts out Chantry Hill to meet the South Downs Way where once again lovely views over the adjoining countryside will be seen.

THE WALK

❶ Walk back to the car park entrance and height barrier, bear left and then turn right and pass by a vehicle barrier. Go ahead on a cart track ignoring a left fork to meet a narrow signed (blue arrow) bridleway. Now follow the fenced bridleway with panoramic northerly views over the countryside. At a crossing bridleway with two field gates to your left press on ahead.

❷ *For the shorter walk:* 100 metres after passing a **trig point** a bridleway is signed to the right. Follow this fenced bridleway between fields to meet a T-junction with the **South Downs Way**. Turn right here along the long-

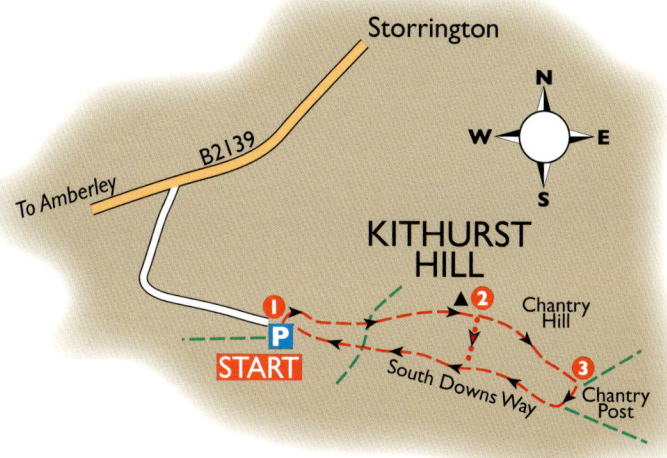

Short Walks in West Sussex

distance path and remain on it to finally meet a vehicle barrier on your right with the car park entrance beyond.

For the longer walk: Ignore this right turn and go ahead through a gate and continue on the narrow path. Soon ignore a path forking left and continue along the rim of **Chantry Hill** with a fence to your right. Pass through a second gate to meet a quiet lane.

❸ Turn right up the steeply rising lane that very soon ends at a rough parking area and the **South Downs Way**. Turn right here along the long-distance path and remain on it to finally meet a vehicle barrier on your right with the car park entrance beyond.

13 West Chiltington & the Nutbourne Vineyard

2 miles (3.2km)

Start: St Mary's Church in Church Street. Roadside parking nearby.
  Postcode: RH20 2JW.
OS Map: OL10 Arundel & Pulborough. **Grid Ref:** TQ091183.
Terrain: Lightly undulating. **Stiles:** 1.
Refreshments: The Rising Sun, Nutbourne, RH20 2HE. ☎ 01798 812191. 🌐 www.facebook.com/The-Rising-Sun-Nutbourne
(At the time of writing the Queens Head pub in West Chiltington was closed and was advertising for a new tenant.)

WALK HIGHLIGHTS

The charming village of West Chiltington is set in the quiet rural idyll below the northern slopes of the South Downs. After beginning beside the village stocks and whipping post by St Mary's Church, the route soon heads off into the scenic countryside beyond. Not long into the walk the way passes through the neat lines of vines of the Nutbourne Vineyard where the panoramic views towards the South Downs are quite stunning. As the way

Short Walks in West Sussex

approaches Lower Jordans farmhouse, it turns and begins to head back to the village where once again superb views are seen as it passes through the vineyard.

THE WALK

❶ Go through the gate of **St Mary's Church** beside the **village stocks** and **whipping post**. Follow a brick path around the right side of the church to soon pass through a gate and continue on a path alongside the graveyard to meet a fingerpost. Turn right here on a narrow path that ends at a road.

❷ Turn left along the road for 20 metres before turning right on a drive signed as a bridleway. Pass a couple of houses and press on along the bridleway to soon meet a fingerpost. Turn left here on the bridleway to meet and pass through a tall gate. Now go ahead through the **Nutbourne Vineyard** on a downwards sloping path.

❸ Continue through a tree-line and go through a gate. Cross a footbridge and follow a fenced path ignoring steps on a right bend. Keep to the path until it ends at steps down to **Lower Jordans Lane**.

❹ Turn right along the lane and at the foot of a slope on a left bend turn right on a track signed as a bridleway. At a gate, press on along the narrower path. After passing stabling, ignore a bridleway to the left and go on up a slope to re-enter the vineyard and meet a fingerpost.

❺ Turn right here between the vines to soon meet your outward path. Turn left and leave the vineyard by following the bridleway. At a T-junction

Walk 13 – **West Chiltington & the Nutbourne Vineyard**

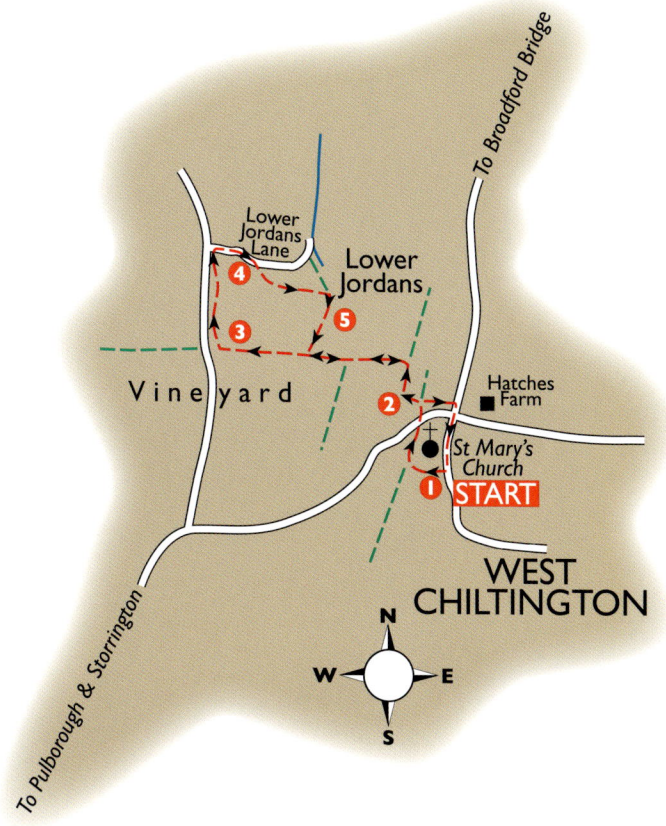

go right to soon re-join the road walked earlier. Turn left and in 20 metres ignore your outward path and continue on the road to soon meet a crossroads where a right turn into **Church Road** brings the route to an end.

14 Rudgwick & Godley's Copse

3 miles (4.8km)

Start: The King's Head, Church Street. Park roadside near the pub or in the pub car park if visiting but please ask the landlord's permission before leaving your car. **Postcode:** RH12 3EA.
OS Map: OL34 Crawley & Horsham. **Grid Ref:** TQ090342.
Terrain: Gently undulating. **Stiles:** None.
Refreshments: The King's Head, RH12 3EB. ☎ 01403 822200.
🌐 www.kingsheadrudgwick.co.uk

WALK HIGHLIGHTS

This lovely rural walk begins and ends beside the King's Head pub that has its origins in the 17th century. The way then passes through the graveyard of Holy Trinity Church that is tucked away behind it. The path continues over fields to meet up with Hermongers Farm. From there the route turns south

Walk 14 – Rudgwick & Godley's Copse

on a cart track before following a bridleway that brings you to Godley's Copse. The path through the copse is easy to follow and a real joy. Later a woodland brook is crossed before meeting a bridleway that leads you past the large house and grounds of Godley's from where its driveway returns you to the outward path to bring this lovely walk to an end.

THE WALK

❶ From the road, seek out a public footpath alongside the southern wall of the **King's Head** pub. Continue through a churchyard on a path to the right of the church and exit via a kissing gate. At a driveway, go left and pass by two cottages. After the second, go ahead on a narrow path and at its end pass through a kissing gate to meet with a crossing track.

❷ Ignore paths to the left and right and go ahead through a gap in the hedge and follow a path through the centre of a field. At the far side, pass through a hedgerow to meet a cart track and follow it through woodland. When buildings are met, press on ahead along a driveway to meet a T-junction.

❸ At this T-junction, turn right along a concrete drive passing some isolated houses and the entrance to **Hermongers Farm**. Keep ahead along the concrete drive. Pass by **Hermongers Barn** and **Little Coopers** and

Short Walks in West Sussex

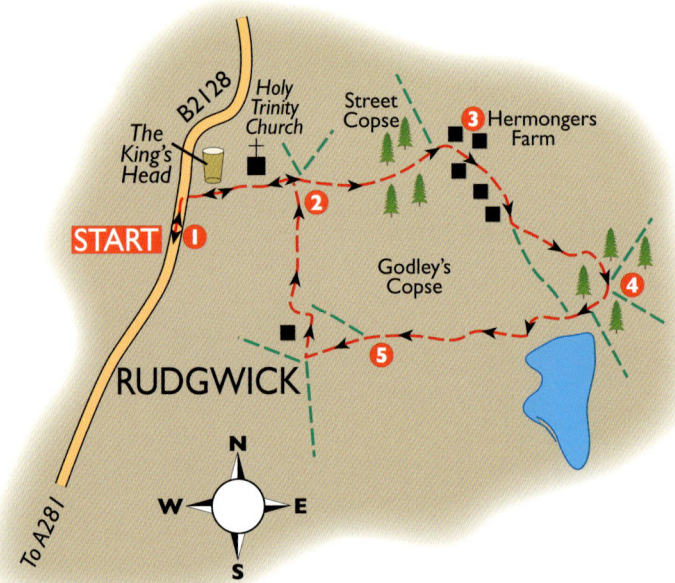

immediately fork left on a signed bridleway. Now follow the bridleway across open fields with far-reaching views.

❹ The bridleway finally enters woodland at a fork. Go right here on a well-trodden path through woodland. The path is ¾ mile (1.2km) long and you should ignore the occasional path to the left and right. Cross a brook and keep to the main path until a fork is reached.

❺ Go left at this fork to soon pass through a gate and 90 metres later meet a crossing bridleway. Turn right along the bridleway to pass by the house and grounds of **Godley's** to meet its driveway. Now follow the driveway until, at a right bend you meet up with your outward path to the left which should be followed to bring this lovely route to its end.

15 The ramparts of Cissbury Ring

2¾ miles (4.4km)

Start: Storrington Rise Car Park, which is signposted from the A24.
  Postcode: BN14 0HT.
OS Map: OL10 Arundel & Pulborough. **Grid Ref:** TQ129077.
Terrain: There is a rise of 360 ft (110m) over the first mile (1.6km) which should not trouble a person of average fitness. **Stiles:** None.
Refreshments: The Gun Inn, Findon, BN14 0TA. ☎ 01903 872235.
🌐 www.thegunfindon.co.uk

WALK HIGHLIGHTS

This stunning walk has outstanding views both inland and over Worthing to the sea beyond. The route makes its way through magnificent countryside below Cissbury Ring before arriving at the eastern entrance of the ancient fortification and the highest point of the route. This is the most historic and largest hillfort in Sussex where the banks and ditches that were excavated some 5,000 years ago are still evident today. After passing through the centre of the fortification the way continues atop the ramparts for a while

Short Walks in West Sussex

before descending over lovely open grassland to return you back to the car park and the end of this good route.

THE WALK

❶ Leave the car park from the right-hand corner furthest from its entrance and go ahead to meet four paths fanning out. Take the left, narrower path and follow it as it goes uphill around the left edge of a meadow. As the path enters woodland it meets a T-junction. Here go left and remain on this path until a gate is met.

❷ Go through the gate and press on along the well trodden path with fine views over **Findon Valley** to the left and **Cissbury Ring** above to the right. Press on to meet a second gate with a wide track beyond. Turn right along the rising track to meet the eastern entrance of **Cissbury hillfort** at the top of the hill.

❸ With a marker post ahead, fork right and go through a kissing gate to enter the hillfort. Ignore steps on either side and go ahead on a grassy path soon ignoring a left fork. Go ahead to a **trig point** and pass to its left. Continue on this grassy path as it curves leftwards and brings you to the western ramparts. Climb steps up the rampart on your right.

❹ Follow the path atop the rampart until steps to your left are met. Go left down the steps, pass through a kissing gate and follow the left-hand path ahead of you down the slope. At an indistinct fork in 120 metres, keep to the

Walk 15 – **The ramparts of Cissbury Ring**

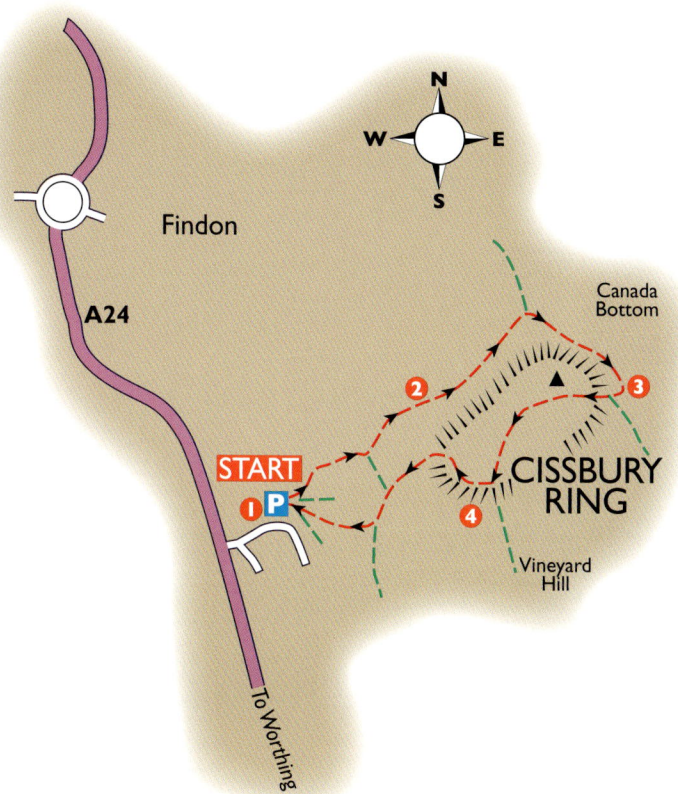

right towards a line of trees. Ignore a kissing gate to your left and go through the gate ahead to meet a large meadow. Go ahead through its centre and when the path passes through a hedgerow, turn right and continue ahead across another grassy meadow to reach the car park beyond.

16 Partridge Green & the River Adur

2½ miles (4km)

Start: The Partridge pub. Park roadside on Meyers Wood road, opposite the frontage of the pub. **Postcode:** RH13 8JN.
OS Map: OL11 Brighton & Hove. **Grid Ref:** TQ189191.
Terrain: Level with just one low rise. **Stiles:** 1.
Refreshments: The Partridge, RH13 8JS. ☎ 01403 710391.
🌐 www.facebook.com/ThePartridgePub

WALK HIGHLIGHTS

This outstanding route begins on the western edge of Partridge Green and very soon the walker will find themself immersed in beautiful open countryside. The route follows well-signed paths alongside level fields and wildflower meadows that lead to the bank of the western branch of the River Adur. Although the route follows the course of the river for a while, only glimpses of the waterway will be seen through the lush foliage that lines its bank. Turning away from the river at Hatterell Bridge the route goes through woodland before continuing alongside a meadow to meet with the Downs Link that returns you to Partridge Green.

Walk 16 – **Partridge Green & the River Adur**

THE WALK

❶ Walk back to the beginning of **Meyers Wood** and cross the road to **The Partridge** pub. Pass by its left side and when by the pub garden cross the road and continue along a tarmac drive towards a house garage. Here pass through a kissing gate on your right and now go left to maintain your original direction alongside a garden. In 30 metres, at a footpath sign, turn left and follow the field edge to the corner.

❷ Turn right here and now follow the field edge to its far end. Turn left for 15 metres and pass through a gate on a signed narrower path between trees. Cross a stile and continue ahead to meet a large field. Turn right along the field edge and follow the grassy path as it swings left to a gate with the river to your left.

❸ Pass through a gate ahead and ignore a footbridge to your left and a path on your right. Now press on ahead along this grassy path to reach **Hatterell Bridge**. Turn right here on a wide track that leads to and through woodland. Press on ahead along the right side of a field and the left side of the next field ahead of you to meet with the **Downs Link**.

Short Walks in West Sussex

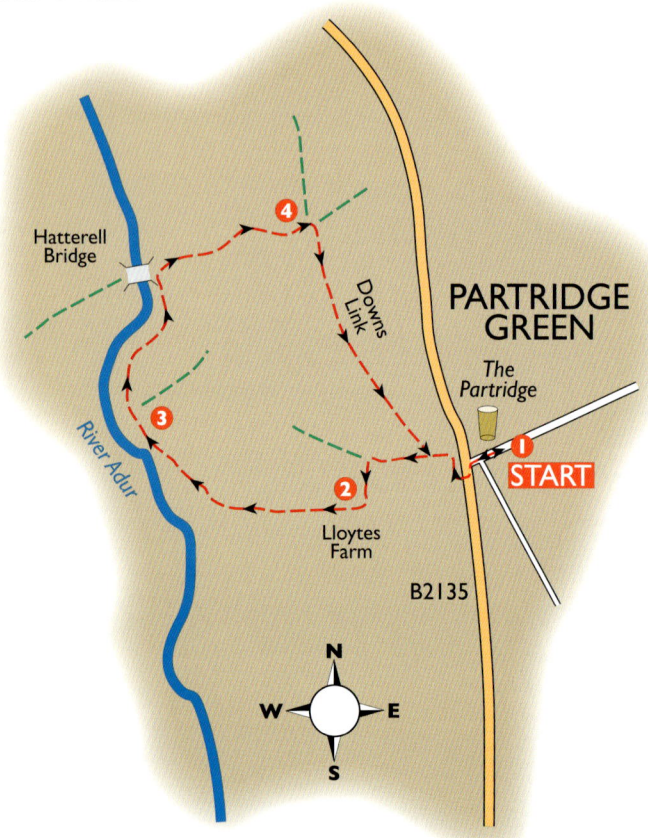

④ Turn right along the **Downs Link** that leads back to **Partridge Green**. Pass by a barrier, turn left and follow your outward path to the end of this good walk.

17 The Downs Link & the River Adur by Henfield

2¾ miles (4.4km)

Start: The small parking area near the Old Railway pub off West End Lane. **Postcode:** BN5 9PJ.
OS Map: OL11 Explorer Brighton & Hove. **Grid Ref:** TQ206162.
Terrain: Fairly level. **Stiles:** None.
Refreshments: The Old Railway, BN5 9PJ. ☎ 01273 492509.
🌐 www.theoldrailwayhenfield.co.uk

WALK HIGHLIGHTS

This lovely route follows the Downs Link; a name derived from the fact that it links the North Downs in Surrey to the South Downs in West Sussex. It is actually a repurposed railway line, 37 miles long, that fell victim to the 'Beeching Cuts' and today is shared by horse riders, cyclists and walkers.

Short Walks in West Sussex

Leaving the path, the way turns south alongside the River Adur. The riverbank offers fine views across open meadows and farmland towards the South Downs in the distance. All too soon the way turns away from the river and follows a path over meadows and along cart tracks to bring you back to the end of this varied route.

THE WALK

❶ The route begins by following the **Downs Link** that adjoins the parking area. Ignore the occasional path to the left and right and stay on the wide path for nearly 1 mile (1.6km).

❷ When railings on both sides of the path are reached, turn left through a kissing gate and follow a path to reach the riverbank. Now go leftwards

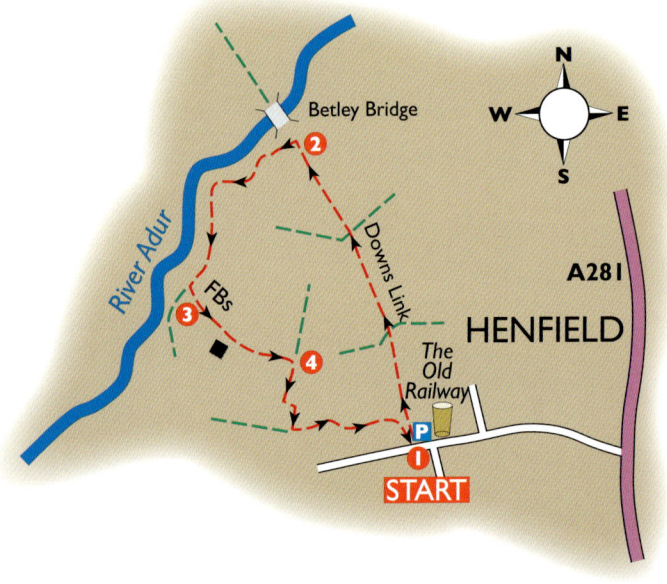

Walk 17 – **The Downs Link & River Adur by Henfield**

alongside the river for ½ mile (0.8km) until a gate across the path is reached by a footpath sign.

❸ The route turns left here away from the river. Follow a grassy path across a meadow crossing two footbridges and press on up a low slope. Keep ahead on the well marked path and press on passing a house. Continue along the track ahead until it ends at a T-junction with another track.

❹ Turn right here and follow it around a bend where another T-junction is met. Now turn left, pass the entrance to a plant nursery and when the track soon turns sharply right, go ahead on a path lined by trees through a pleasing modern development of homes. At the end of the path, turn right to soon rejoin the small parking area and the end of this route.

18 Balcombe & The Warren

3¼ miles (5.2 km)

Start: Stockcroft Road in the centre of Balcombe. Park at the roadside near the Victory Hall. **Postcode:** RH17 6HP.
OS Map: OS Explorer 135 Ashdown Forest. **Grid Ref:** TQ309306.
Terrain: Easy and undulating. **Stiles:** 4, not dog friendly.
Refreshments: The Half Moon Inn, Balcombe, RH17 6PA.
☎ 01444 811582. 🌐 www.halfmoonbalcombe.com

WALK HIGHLIGHTS

This scenic walk in the High Weald Area of Outstanding Natural Beauty begins in the heart of Balcombe village before passing the cricket ground to reach picturesque Balcombe Lake and its reflective waters. After crossing a couple of fields and passing Forest Farm, a quiet lane is reached which

Walk 18 – **Balcombe & The Warren**

will lead you to a track that passes through The Warren on a lovely level woodland track. As the route begins its return, a boardwalk over a spring is crossed from where a field path leads back to the village.

THE WALK

❶ From where you have parked, walk to the **Half Moon Inn** and pass its frontage to meet the gateway of **Balcombe House**. Here follow the track right that passes between fields to meet a bend at the bottom of the slope. Go ahead into a cricket ground and follow the boundary left to meet and continue on a well-trodden path through woodland.

❷ At the end of woodland, pass through a gate and turn right along a downhill field edge to meet and cross a footbridge over a brook to enter a second field. Go diagonally left towards a hedgerow and cross a stile to join a lane. Turn left to meet the drive of **Woodward's Farm** at a sharp right bend. Continue ahead along the farm drive passing **Balcombe Lake** along the way.

❸ Remain on the drive for ½ mile (.8km) until, after climbing a rise and following the drive around a left bend, you cross a stile on your right beside a field gate. Go ahead along the field edge to its end. Turn left over a stile and go ahead on an indistinct grassy path to the top corner of the field. Turn right into the next field keeping a hedgerow to your right with the buildings of **Forest Farm** seen on the brow of the hill ahead and left. At the farm drive, go ahead to meet a quiet country lane.

❹ Turn left along the lane and later ignore a signed footpath on your left by a passing place. Soon after, turn left on a signed footpath along a private drive marked **Paddockhurst Estate**. Pass a couple of cottages, go through a gate and follow the track through woodland for almost 1 mile (1.6km).

❺ After leaving woodland a large field is passed on your right. At the second field seen to your right go through a gate ahead and, when on a slight downhill slope in the track, look out for a signed footpath to your left.

❻ Turn left down steps before turning right and continuing along a planked boardwalk across springs. At the end, climb steps and follow the path ahead

Short Walks in West Sussex

through woodland. Ignore a path to your left and keep ahead to a kissing gate and enter a field. Press on along the right-hand field edge to eventually meet the track walked earlier. Turn right and retrace your steps back into the village centre.

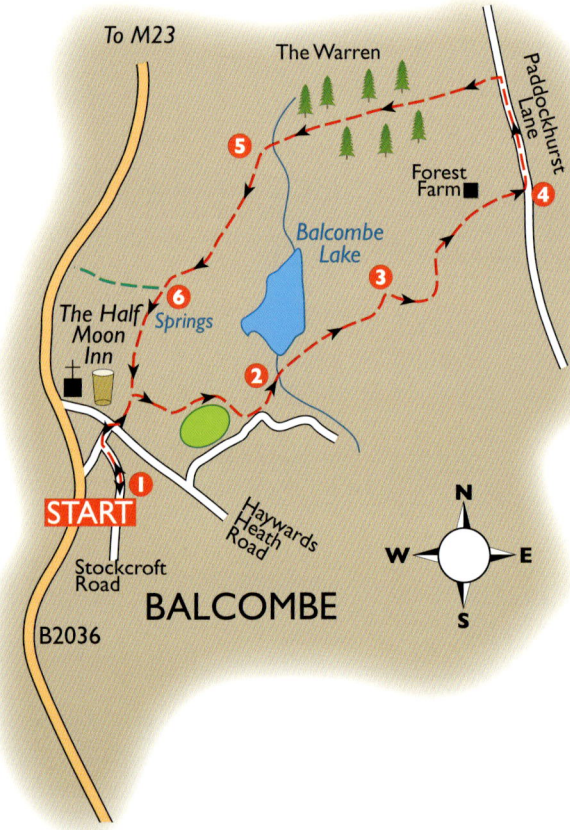

19 Hurstpierpoint & Cutlers Brook

2 miles (3.2km)

Start: Brown Twins Road Car Park. **Postcode:** BN6 9PA.
OS Map: OL11 Brighton & Hove. **Grid Ref:** TQ284165.
Terrain: Fairly level. **Stiles:** 4, all dog friendly.
Refreshments: The Poacher, BN6 9PU. ☎ 01273 834202.
🌐 No website.

WALK HIGHLIGHTS

This charming walk begins and ends in Hurstpierpoint's High Street with its good array of shops. After leaving the village centre behind, the route immerses itself in the countryside to its south. Easily followed paths and tracks are all well signposted and will guide you through peaceful meadows which are set against the backdrop of the South Downs in the distance. The route twice crosses footbridges over Cutlers Brook, a tributary to the River Adur before making its return to the centre of the village.

Short Walks in West Sussex

THE WALK

❶ Follow the signed path leftwards to meet the **High Street**. Now turn right along the pavement to a pedestrian crossing and cross the road. Go right and in 20 metres turn left into **Pit Lane** and follow it until it ends.

❷ Go ahead on a narrow path alongside a wall. The path continues between fenced fields and crosses **Cutlers Brook** via a footbridge. Go ahead over a grassy area to meet a drive. Go left along the drive to its end.

❸ Cross a stile and press on along a well-trodden path beside a fenced field and cross a stile at its end. Continue ahead and pass a massive oak tree, taking care of the roots that conspire to trip. Keep ahead on the path and soon pass through a kissing gate.

❹ Keep ahead, go through a squeeze stile and press on to a line of trees and a fingerpost. Turn left here along the field edge to soon pass through trees and meet another meadow. Continue ahead, pass through a kissing gate, cross **Cutlers Brook** via a sturdy bridge and keep on to meet a drive and another fingerpost.

Walk 19 – **Hurstpierpoint & Cutlers Brook**

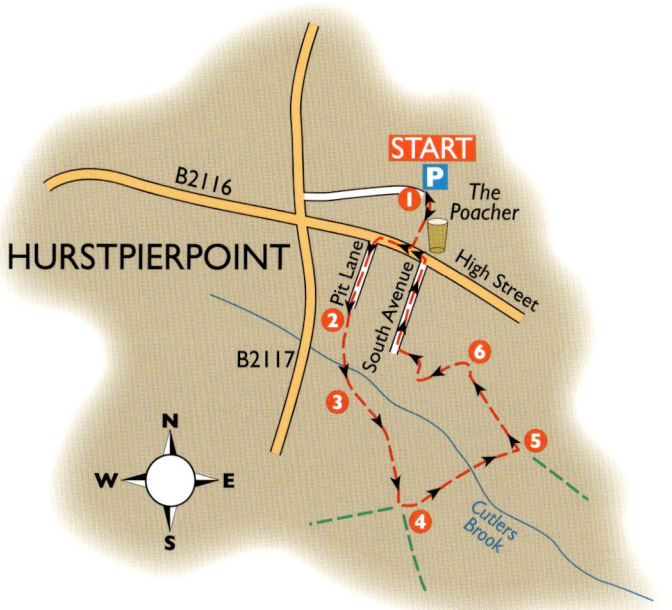

⑤ Turn left here over a meadow and pass through a kissing gate. Continue ahead through the next meadow and pass through a second kissing gate. Keep ahead to meet a cart track, ignore a field gate ahead and turn left along the track. When the track bends left, turn right over a stile and continue along the edge of a meadow.

⑥ At the corner of the meadow, pass through a kissing gate and go left on a fenced path to meet **South Avenue**. Turn right along the pavement to rejoin the **High Street**. Cross the road with caution; turn left and pass the **Players Theatre** where the path back to the car park will be soon met beside **The Poacher** pub.

20 Crawley Down & the Sussex Border Path

3½ miles (5.6km)

Start: Station Road in the centre of the village where there is a choice of two car parks. **Postcode:** RH10 4HZ.
OS Map: OS Explorer 135 Ashdown Forest. **Grid Ref:** TQ347374.
Terrain: Gently undulating. **Stiles:** 1, dog friendly.
Refreshments: The Crown At Turners Hill, RH10 4PT. ☎ 01342 715218.

WALK HIGHLIGHTS

Crawley Down village is tucked into the northeast corner of West Sussex and nestles between the large towns of Crawley and East Grinstead. This super route follows field paths to the south of the village that lead you through

Walk 20 – Crawley Down & the Sussex Border Path

scenic rolling countryside and passes between the picturesque mill ponds at Fen Place Mill and along well signed paths through its pristine grounds. The route then heads for the fields of Tilkhurst Farm where the way meets the Sussex Border Path from where it makes its return on the long-distance path back into the village to complete this good circuit.

THE WALK

❶ From either car park, when facing the small parade of shops, go left alongside the road to meet **Sandhill Lane**, a private road signed as a public footpath. Go ahead on this quiet road and later ignore a right fork. Continue ahead along **Burleigh Lane** until it ends at the gates of **Burleigh House Farm**. Here, go ahead through a kissing gate to the left and continue along the path.

❷ Look out for a fingerpost. Turn right here and follow a grassy path to a kissing gate. Ignore a path to the left and continue ahead. Soon pass between two large picturesque mill ponds and follow the well-signed path. Pass the gates to **Fen Place Mill** and press on alongside a barn to meet a track.

Short Walks in West Sussex

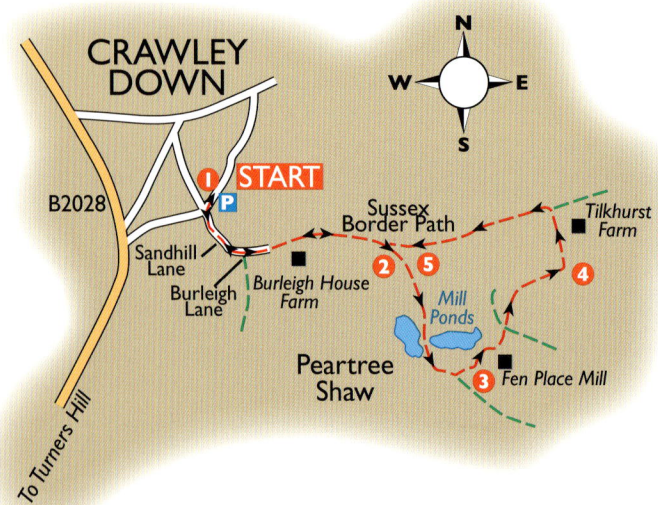

3 Turn left along the track before soon turning right as directed. Go left as directed and cross a footbridge over a stream. Keep ahead to another fingerpost and turn right. The path now enters woodland where you should ignore a stile on your right. The path ends at a dog-friendly stile which you cross. Now continue ahead alongside a large field.

4 Halfway along the field follow the path left, cross a footbridge and enter a second field. Continue up a slope and at the top, pass through a hedgerow and press on ahead to meet a well-trodden crossing path. This is the **Sussex Border Path** and here you turn left and follow it to the end of the field.

5 Pass through a kissing gate and press on through others before the path goes up a slope between newly planted tree saplings to meet a fingerpost and your outward path. Go ahead here and retrace your steps back to the village centre and the end of this good circuit.